BUILDINGS FOR BOOKS

Chris van Uffelen

BUILDINGS FOR BOOKS

Contemporary
Library
Architecture

BRAUN

CONTENTS

Libraries all over the world are places of knowledge and culture. They keep books, libri in Latin, as objects, and they keep the contents of these books: Pages filled with letters and illustrations on a first level; drama, comedy, history, science and faith on a second. But also manuscripts and music collections, art libraries and nowadays even data collections, especially e-books, belong to their collection areas.

When we speak of libraries here, this primarily means public or at least semi-public collections, even though their history began with archives and private libraries. The collecting and indexing of documents in one place began with the Sumerians and their clay tablets with cuneiform writing in 2600 B.C. Manuscript collections in private libraries followed in ancient Greece in the 5th century B.C. The important library of Alexandria originated in the 3rd century B.C. The book as a bound multi-page object then probably began its triumphal procession as a codex – originally as a stack of wooden or wax tablets – from the first century A.D. onwards, and acquired the form that is still common today in the 4th century A.D. Of course, it was still in manuscript, and throughout the Middle Ages it was mainly produced in the scriptoriums of the monasteries. For large editions, in Tang Dynasty China (615-906), woodblock printing was already used, which had half or full pages on a carrier medium. Such single-page woodblock prints were bound into block books in Europe from 1400 as well, and remained popular for centuries.

After this, Johannes Gensfleisch, known as Gutenberg, brought about a printing revolution in Mainz around 1450 that changed the world forever: letterpress printing with movable type enabled cost-effective fast production of small editions by recycling the individual letters. And he made it possible to work out the individual letters in better quality, in a particularly practical alloy of tin, lead and antimony. In addition, he invented a new oil-based black printing ink and a printing press – a complete production line for books with identical text. That is – at least for the actual book block: Binding was a different craft at the time and was commissioned separately. In 1997, the American magazine Time-Life declared Gutenberg to be the most important inventor of the second millennium. Until 1500, about 30,000 so-called incunabula (Latin: birthplace, cradle) were produced using various printing techniques, bound or not. Another important step towards the spread of the book medium followed in 1799 with the invention of the paper machine.

Since then, thanks in part to the literacy of the general population, books have conquered the world, spread knowledge, provided enlightenment and sparked revolutions. The Harry Potter volumes alone have reached a worldwide circulation of over 500 million copies.

Back to the public libraries. Here, too, there was probably already a first one in Greek antiquity: Peisistratos, of all people, who had himself proclaimed tyrant in 561 BC, most likely founded it in Athens. However, the first public collections of importance to us were those, at the beginning of the 17th century, of the Bodleian Library in Oxford and the Biblioteca Ambrosiana in Milan, which opened their reading rooms to the general public. Most libraries, however, remained reserved for students, and even today it is the university libraries that – along with the monastic libraries – guard the most extensive knowledge. They occupy an adequate space in this publication. The real boom of public libraries began in the 19th century. In this volume there are also updates of such older institutions. For today, they all must deal with new media, must serve new reading habits, take up new media consumption concepts. However, the question of whether they will also develop into archives for social media or whether they will concentrate on their core competence of "printed matter" due to the masses of data must remain open for the time being.

Gutenberg Bible
around 1455

Bibliothèque nationale de France

The Bookworm
by Carl Spitzweg, detail

Version of 1851

Oil on canvas

48.2 × 26.6 cm

Grohmann Museum on loan from

the Milwaukee Public Library

Gutenberg Bible
around 1455

Bibliothèque nationale de France

Project ZIKAWEI LIBRARY
Shanghai <u>Architecture</u> Wutopia Lab <u>Address</u>
Xuhui District, Shanghai, China <u>Client</u> Xuhui
District Administration of Culture and
Tourism, Xuhui District Library <u>Completion</u>
2022 <u>Size</u> 18,650 m² <u>Type of library</u> Public
<u>Reading seats</u> 800 <u>Original building</u> David
Chipperfield Architects, 2022

b

In the Zikawei library, Wutopia Lab created a 'Chinese nested box'-structure, which is derived from the traditional Chinese trousseau box in the Han Dynasty. The first layer is the thin façade, the second consists of the main programs of the library such as various reading areas, lecture halls etc., the third layer is the donut-shaped aisle, the fourth is the atrium that serves as the library's reading hall, and lastly, the heart of the library: the pagoda from the Tou-Se-We Museum. Leading to it is the nearly 30 meters long reading table. Together they both reinforce the central axis. The atrium was designed to be a warm lighted open space that welcomes people. Nevertheless there are places of retreat for reading, such as the step seating area.

e

cd

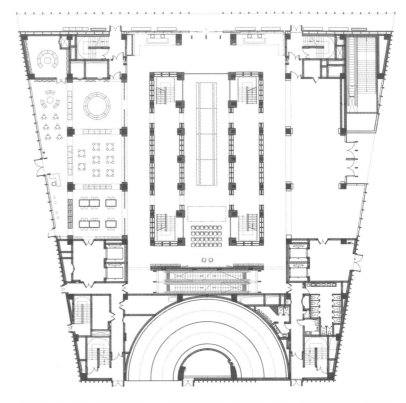

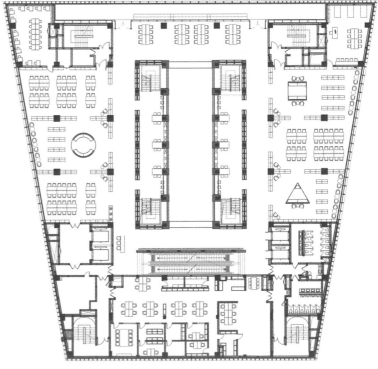

F

Project CENTRAL LIBRARY NEUDE
Utrecht <u>Architecture</u> Zecc Architecten
<u>Address</u> Neude 11, 3512 AE Utrecht, the
Netherlands <u>Client</u> Utrecht Library <u>Completion</u>
2020 <u>Size</u> 9,000 m² <u>Type of library</u> Public
<u>Reading seats</u> 600 <u>Original building</u> Joop
Crouwel, post office, 1924

a

b
Permanent collection and
escalators.

c
Children's collection with
reading room
d
Study hall under the wooden
roof construction

13

The library in the style of the Amsterdam School has a phenomenal central hall with a wealth of form, light and artisan use of materials. Zecc Architecten together with Rijnboutt architects transformed this hall into a vibrant square and an extension piece of the city. From the central hall six new openings above the historical doors offer new sources of light. The escalators lead to the various floors. Walking through the library resembles a voyage of discovery through special rooms and areas: from the traditional library to the playfully structured children's department. There are also study areas which are enclosed with modern glass walls. Through the new roof window you can enjoy the panorama of the old city center of Utrecht.

b

c d

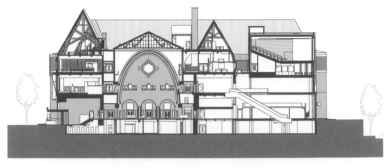

ef

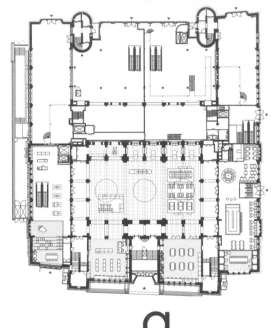

g

h

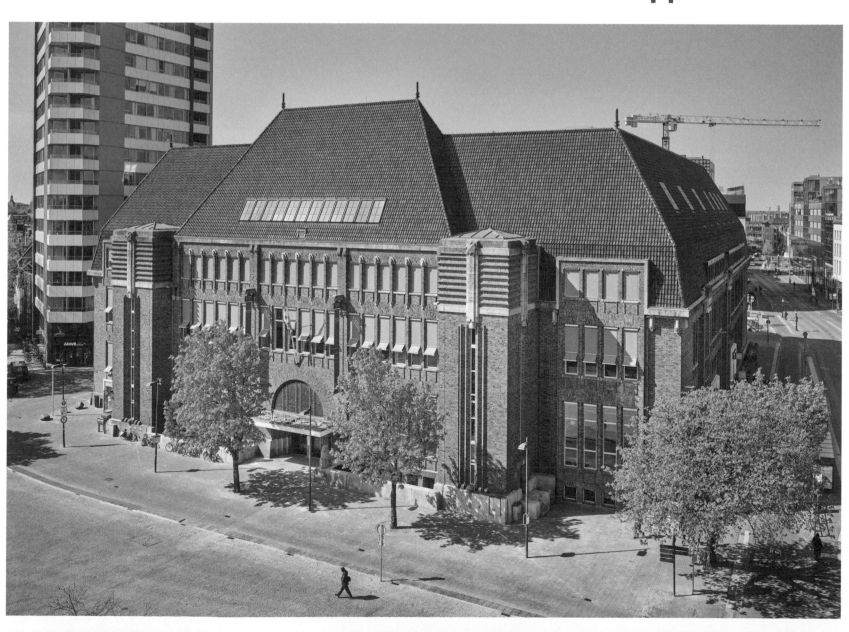

Project DEICHMAN BJØRVIKA
Oslo Architecture Lundhagem; Atelier Oslo
architects Interior Scenario Address Anne
Cath Vestlys plass 1, 0150 Oslo, Norway Client
Municipality of Oslo Completion 2020 Size
19,600 m² Type of library Public, with Deichman
Collection Reading seats 1200

a

This library is an environmentally friendly building. Innovative solutions are used for the façade, ventilation and materials. To avoid building too many floors, the building cantilevers over its footprint. To create a greater sense of openness the ground floor façade is fully transparent. Three light shafts cut diagonally through the building from each of the entrances. The light shafts connect the floors and distribute daylight downward from three large skylights in the roof. An open public space dominates the interior, with a variety of furniture and activities. Enclosed spaces and niches are organized around three free-standing book towers. The concrete structures are durable elements that give the building a lasting and recognizable quality.

b

c

de

f

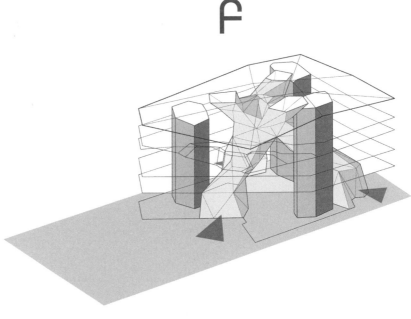

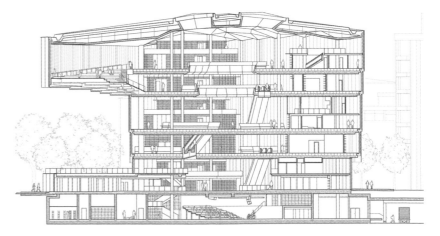

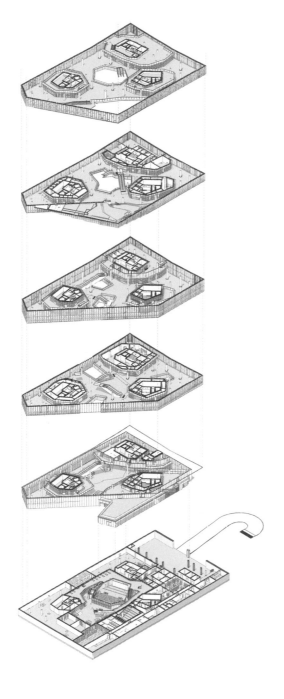

g

h

Project UNIVERSITY OF SEMNAN AUDITORIUM AND LIBRARY
Semnan Architecture New Wave Architecture
Address JC3P+F5F, Semnan, Iran Client
University of Semnan Completion 2023 Size
14,000 m² Type of library University

a

b

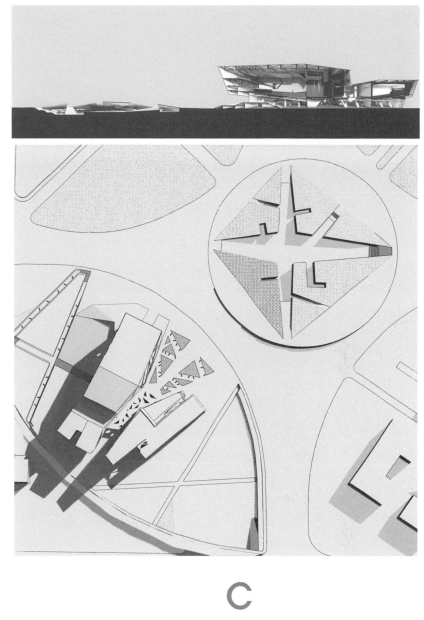

c

The avant-garde architecture of Semnan University is inspired by traditional Iranian motifs, particularly evident in the intricate openings and ribbons applied to the façade, which adorn the building, reflect Iran's rich cultural and artistic heritage, and allow for the use of natural light. The façade is designed as an integrated part of the building's architecture and structure. The complex contains two separate volumes: a library and an auditorium, which are connected by a corridor that allows ample light to enter the building. The windows are irregular triangular openings that bring natural light into the building and provide natural ventilation. The turquoise color is inspired by traditional Iranian art and creates a familiar feeling for the users.

de

f

g

<u>Project</u> NEW TAIPEI CITY LIBRARY TAISHAN
BRANCH
Taipei <u>Architecture</u> A.C.H Architects <u>Interior</u>
Atelier Cube <u>Address</u> 5F, No. 212, Quanxing Road,
New Taipei City, Taiwan <u>Client</u> New Taipei City
Library <u>Completion</u> 2023 <u>Size</u> 1,320 m² <u>Type of</u>
<u>library</u> Public, with Multimedia <u>Reading seats</u>
100 <u>Original building</u> 2004

a

Founded 20 years ago, the library is located on the 5th floor of a government building in Taishan District, New Taipei City. The single-story library has an open design and consists of several functional areas. It uses the high ceilings of the building to create a series of unique bookcase designs. Open wooden shelving with hollow planks create a conceptual forest. A continuity of transparent materiality and see-through design creates a poetic visual unity and interactive environment. In addition, the number of visitors to the library has increased by 50 percent, and the use of the children's reading area has more than tripled since the renovation.

b

cd

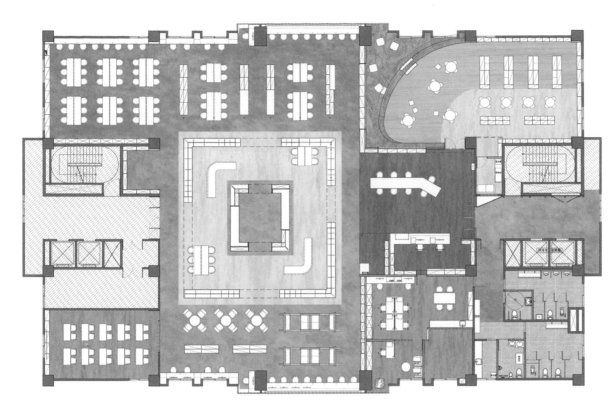

f

g

STAVROS NIARCHOS
FOUNDATION LIBRARY

New York City, NY

Mecanoo and Beyer
Blinder Belle Architects

a
Long room exterior

28

Project STAVROS NIARCHOS FOUNDATION LIBRARY
New York City, NY Architecture Mecanoo and Beyer Blinder Belle Architects & Planners Address 455 5th Avenue, New York City, NY, USA Client New York Public Library Completion 2021 Size 16,722 m² Type of library Public, with Multimedia and Music

a

b

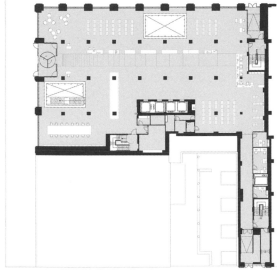

c d

The Stavros Niarchos Foundation Library (SNFL) is a new-generation library for all New Yorkers. The design includes long tables of impressive scale, ceiling artwork in the long room and the use of classic materials including natural stone, terrazzo, and oak. SNFL's ground floor is arranged around an internal street that runs beneath a floating linear canopy of wood beams, from the Fifth Avenue entrance to the welcome desks. Located on one side are elevators, stairs, and a mezzanine balcony. On the other side, a rectangular opening in the floor plate reveals the lower ground floor, which houses a children's library and teen center. The children's library play area enjoys natural light, and the teen center has a dedicated staircase.

e

f g

h

Project MIRURU NASUSHIOBARA CITY LIBRARY
Nasushiobara <u>Architecture</u> UAO <u>Lighting</u> Izumi
Okayasu <u>Landscape</u> Studio Terra <u>Address</u> 1-1
Honcho, Nasushiobara, Tochigi 325-0056, Japan
<u>Client</u> City of Nasushiobara <u>Completion</u> 2020
<u>Size</u> 4,968 m² <u>Type of library</u> Public <u>Reading
seats</u> 408

a

In Nasushiobara the public library and plaza are fluidly integrated into the surroundings of the train station. The library was planned to serve as a community center, where people could be drawn directly from the station plaza. The architecture, inspired by the shape of a forest, creates an ecological experience of mutual inspiration and succeeds in creating an optimal library environment as a place for lifelong learning. An atrium connects the busy ground floor with the comfortable and quiet first floor. The ceiling is inspired by the shape of leaf lines. It controls the natural sunlight from the skylights, creating an ever-changing light environment.

b

cd

MIRURU NASUSHIOBARA
CITY LIBRARY

e
Bookshelves and group
workspaces
f
Glass façade by night

g
Section, second floor and
ground floor plan

34

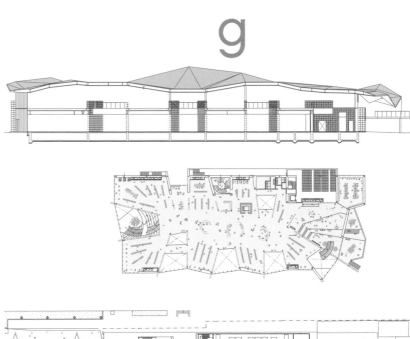

g

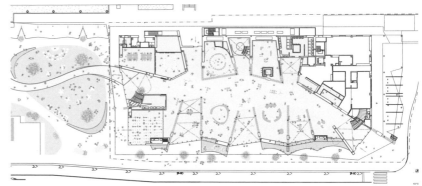

ef

h

Project BAYEUX MEDIA LIBRARY
Bayeux Architecture Serero Architectes
Address 1, boulevard Fabien Ware, 14400 Bayeux,
France Client Bayeux Intercom Completion 2019
Size 2,550 m² Type of library Public Reading
seats 250

a

Located on the ring road around the dense center of Bayeux, the new Bayeux Media Library is thoughtfully integrated into the city's rich historical context. The project is built on an open site that links the historic center with the city's future development zones, creating a magnificent view of the cathedral. This exceptional situation required a very careful treatment, with the architect choosing to propose a transparent, landscaped building as a true urban showcase. The project design expresses an open relationship between the inside and the outside, with the patio and the outdoor reading terraces on the south side open to the media library's various uses and users.

b

c

de

f

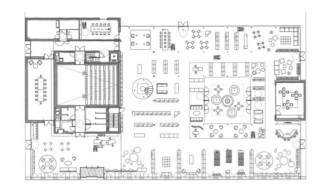

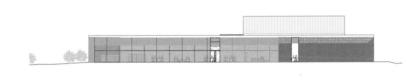

h

g

Project WINTHROP LIBRARY
Winthrop, WA Architecture Johnston
Architects; Prentiss Balance Wickline
Architects Landscape Karen Kiest | Landscape
Architects Address 112 Norfolk Road, Winthrop,
WA 98862, USA Client Friends of Winthrop
Library Completion 2022 Size 678 m² Type of
library Public Reading seats 64

a

b

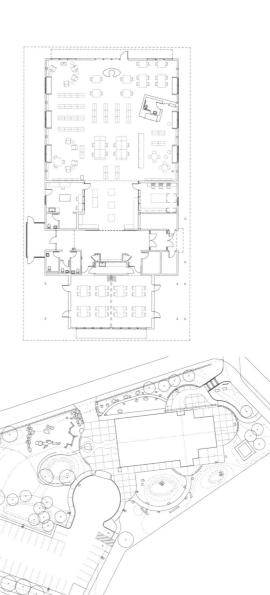

c

The library is in the Methow Valley. The architects held charettes with patrons to collect comments about community needs that were later incorporated into the design. Inspired by the agrarian buildings in the region, it includes broad overhangs and open roof trusses, and the massing suits the community's aesthetic. The building includes spaces for lectures, meetings, and a makerspace provides 3D printers and sewing machines. Computers, printers, and free internet are available. The library is the result of public/private partnerships: The land was donated by the Town of Winthrop, Washington State gave part of the money, while volunteers at Friends of Winthrop Library (FOWL) raised money with more than 1,000 donors.

de

fg

h

Project SPRINGDALE LIBRARY & KOMAGATA
MARU PARK
Brampton Architecture RDHA Address 10705
Bramalea Road, Brampton, ON L6R 0C1 Canada
Client City of Brampton Completion 2019 Size
2,418 m² Type of library Public Reading seats
100

a

ხ

In the City of Brampton the Springdale Library and Komagata Maru Park provides the suburban community with a new public library and community park. RDHA's goal was to create an inclusive gathering place, a counterpoint to the otherwise flat suburban area, and a point of pride for the city. The project site was physically constrained, framed by a commercial plaza to the east, a main road to the south, and a natural ravine to the north and west. The architects positioned the library as close to the street as possible, in order to solidify the building's presence with the street, preserve the site's natural topography and irrigation patterns, and channel interior views towards the ravine.

C

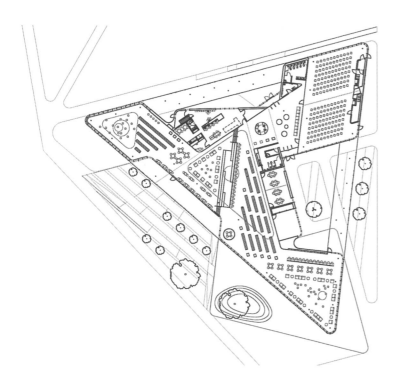

d

e f

Project LEA BRIDGE LIBRARY PAVILION
London **Architecture** Studio Weave **Landscape**
Tom Massey, Studio Weave **Address** Lea
Bridge Road, London E10 7HU, UK **Client** London
Borough of Waltham Forest **Completion** 2021
Size 250 m² **Type of library** Public **Reading seats**
25+ **Original building** William Jacques, 1905

a

h
Ground floor plan

c
Pavilion and glass facade
d
Workspace with outward view
and pavilion

49

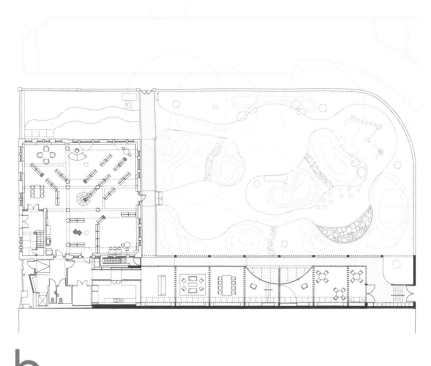

b

c d

Studio Weave were commissioned to design an extension to the Lea Bridge Library in London, adding a cafe and adaptable community space to deliver a revived civic heart for the Borough of Waltham Forest. The project addresses the changing role of a library in modern civic infrastructure, conceiving a new wing that offers places to work, learn, socialize, and gather. The scheme adjoins to the rear of the original Edwardian red brick library, lightly engaging with the listed setting, and features materiality which complements the tonality of its forebear. To achieve both a sympathetic site layout and structural efficiency, the extension leans against a blank perpendicular party wall, from which the new wing enjoys panoramic views of the garden.

e

f

g

h

LIBRIO YUKUHASHI   Yukuhashi   Kazuhiko Mashiko &   a   52
                                             MIKAMI Architects   Facility with a large pilotis
                                                                       space facing main street

Project LIBRIO YUKUHASHI
Yukuhashi Architecture Kazuhiko Mashiko
& MIKAMI Architects Address 3-18-1 Ohashi,
Yukuhashi, Japan Client City of Yukuhashi
Completion 2020 Size 5,143 m² Type of library
Public Reading seats 580

a

The name Yukuhashi comes from a merger of two former villages through the municipal system: the former Gyoji Village and the former Ohashi Village. The planned site of the project was positioned along the right bank of the Nagao River on the boundary between the two former villages, while repairing and preserving their townscape areas. The twisted framework is based on a response to the local and historical character of the area while generously encompassing the required functions. The framework will live on, even if the functions eventually change to suit the times, and the architecture will weave a new story within the historical context of the site.

b

c

b
Second floor children's reading
area

c
Atrium of first and second floor

d
Third floor studying area next
to the Nagao River
e
Interior covered with metal
louvers

d e

f

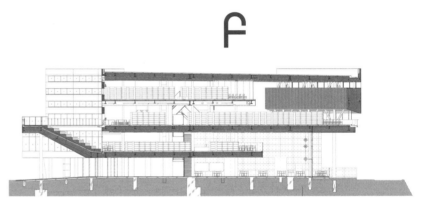

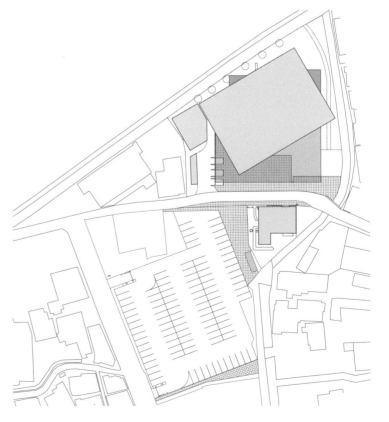

g

Project CITY LIBRARY WALDSHUT
Waldshut-Tiengen Architecture UKW
Innenarchitekten Signage atelier-werk Address
Bismarckstraße 12, 79761 Waldshut-Tiengen,
Germany Client City of Waldshut-Tiengen
Completion 2022 Size 545 m² Type of library
Public Reading seats 90 Original building
Thomas Cathiau, 1862

a

b c

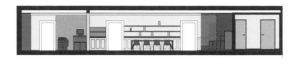

d

The representative Kornhaus Waldshut, built in 1862, is a listed building and serves many cultural functions. The first and second floors house the city library. Despite the extensive renovations that were necessary, much of the historic charm has been preserved. Today, the library is open 98 hours a week for events and as a place to study. It is completely barrier-free. New elements such as the colorful, monolithic staircase with seating and the new flooring of native silver fir dominate the space and create a positively inspiring atmosphere.

g

ef

h

Project NOT JUST LIBRARY
Taipei City Architecture JC. Architecture &
Design Landscape Motif Planning & Design
Consultants Address No. 133, Guangfu S
Road, Taipei City, Taiwan Client Taiwan Design
Research Institute Completion 2020 Size
212 m² Type of library Public Reading seats 100
Original building Bath house, 1937

a

h
Main reading 'pool', with bookcases that can be converted
into seating

61

'Not Just Library' is an embodiment of a cultural oa-
sis that revitalizes the decades-old bathhouse into a
space where inner creativity and knowledge are em-
braced. This is where, amidst gentle lights and raw materials, lovers of printed works arrive to immerse in the
scent of books, the pond of pages, and the garden of
words. Birch plywood bookshelves and the arched bath's
vintage white-tile mottled walls are where heritage
is preserved and highlighted to express timelessness.
Adorned by native Taiwanese plants, the garden radiates tranquility outward, peacefully telling the story
of transitioning in time as juxtaposed to the liveliness
of Taipei.

b

c
Original 85-year-old bathhouse
d
Bookshelves in front of the old
window frames

e
Ground floor plan

c d

e

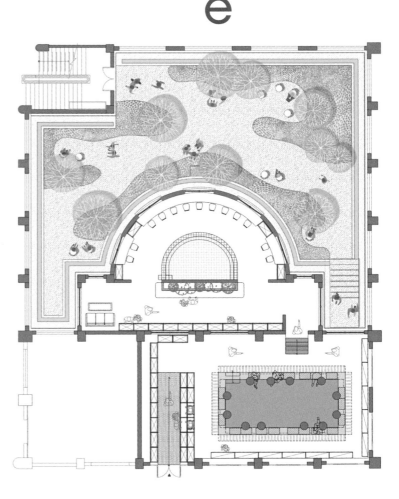

F

STADTBIBLIOTHEK IM
MOTORAMA

Munich

CBA Clemens Bachmann
Architekten

a
Computer area

64

Project STADTBIBLIOTHEK IM MOTORAMA
Munich Architecture CBA Clemens Bachmann
Architekten Address Rosenheimer Straße
30–32, 81669 Munich, Germany Client Gasteig
München GmbH Completion 2021 Size 3,600 m²
Type of library Public Reading seats 105

a

The interim library is situated in Motorama, a shopping center connected to a train station, making it a highly public place. The different departments were planned in the former store units, each of which can be opened to the large corridor via sliding glass elements. The coolness and anonymity of the existing architecture was countered by a differentiated color concept to distinguish the departments. Like patches of color on a white canvas, the entrances and rooms for the subunits stand out from the monotonous white-gray context. This way, the visitor is immersed in the respective color worlds and is emotionally stimulated in the process. Industrial, low-cost materials complement the image of a temporary, experimental library.

b

c

d

ef

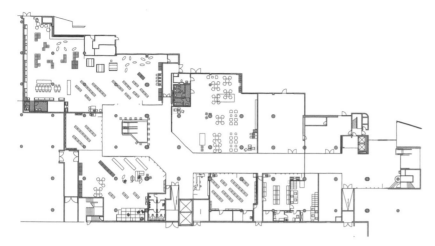

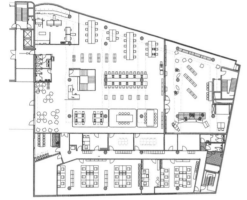

g

h

Project VIBY LIBRARY AND CULTURE HOUSE
Copenhagen **Architecture** CCO Architects
Address Bragesgade 10 A, Copenhagen,
Denmark **Client** Municipality of Roskilde
Completion 2021 **Size** 1,400 m² **Type of library**
Public **Reading seats** 25

a

b c

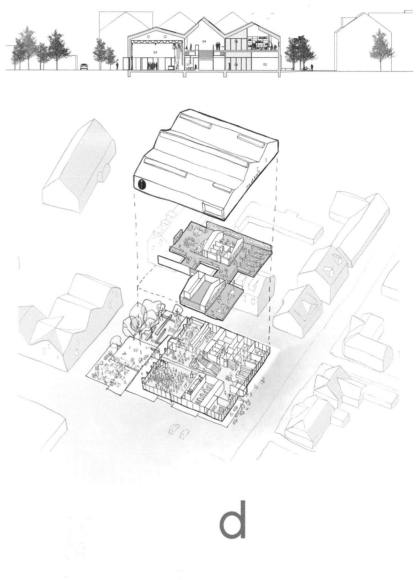

d

The overall architectural concept of the Viby Library and Culture House is a modern take on the nordic common house typology, which provided an extension to people's homes. It was built to create a new living room for the town. The ground floor holds citizen services, café, and flex-room for workshops. The library is located on the first floor. For the interior, the choices are a mix of clean white surfaces combined with clear color floors and wooden surfaces to highlight certain areas. This is exemplified in the characteristic inbuilt wooden bookcases and the special ceramic café desk that creates a tactile and inviting atmosphere, whereas the all-black multi-space creates an atmosphere of focus and concentration.

e

fg

h

THE GOLDEN HORN
LIBRARY

Istanbul

Aytaç Architects

a
Library entry view from
the metro station

72

Project THE GOLDEN HORN LIBRARY
Istanbul Architecture Aytaç Architects
Address Azapkapi, 34421, Beyoglu, Istanbul,
Turkey Client Istanbul Metropolitan
Municipality Completion 2023 Size 4,515 m² Type
of library Public Reading seats 283

a

c

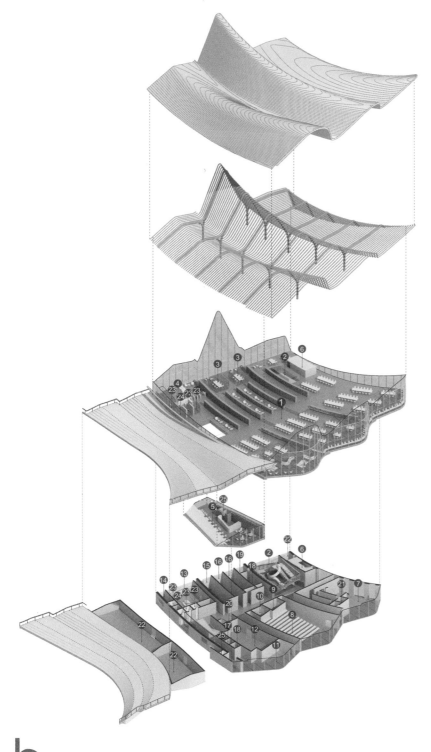

b

The Golden Horn Library is located on the other side of the historical peninsula overlooking the seven hills of Istanbul. The project aims to be a means of connecting the symbols of the city. It radiates the energy to the city instead of directing all the energy to itself. The library has been conceived almost as a floating Turkish carpet. The axiality of the seven hills facing the Galata Tower formed the roofscape that houses all the functions of the library. The building is designed to blend in with its surrounding through a smooth transition. The Library Learning Center is elevated to create a calm atmosphere and the noisy ground floor houses all the services, including an auditorium, a spiral-shaped children's library and a restaurant.

d

e

f

Project <u>CULTURE STATION</u>
Rumia <u>Architecture</u> Sikora Interiors <u>Address</u>
Starowiejska 2, 84-230 Rumia, Poland <u>Client</u>
Municipal Public Library Rumia <u>Completion</u> 2014
<u>Size</u> 1,763 m² <u>Type of library</u> Public <u>Reading</u>
<u>seats</u> 150 <u>Original building</u> 1960

a

b

The Culture Station was officially opened in September 2014. In addition to serving as a station for mostly suburban trains, it now also functions as a modern and elegant cultural center. Culture Station began to organize many cultural events, such as exhibitions, theater and film workshops, and author readings. Its premises include a library and reading room, conference rooms, different workshops and space for children. The architectural design is a harmonious synthesis of modernity and coziness, combining austerity and functionality with the use of warm colors and wood finishes. The character of the interior is further enhanced by various decorative accents that refer to railway traditions.

C

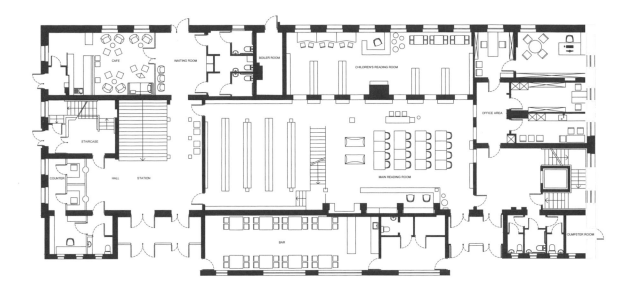

e

d

WAUNAKEE PUBLIC
LIBRARY

Waunakee, WI

OPN Architects

a
Library complimenting the
landscape

80

Project WAUNAKEE PUBLIC LIBRARY
Waunakee, WI Architecture OPN Architects
Landscape Confluence Address 201 N. Madison
Street, Waunakee, WI 53597, USA Client Village
of Waunakee Completion 2019 Size 3,720 m²
Type of library Public

a

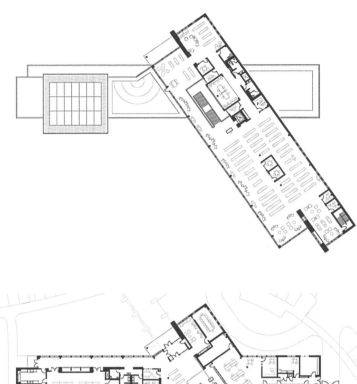

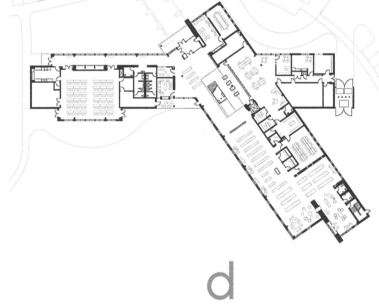

b c

d

This vibrant, multipurpose 40,000-square-foot public library serves as a space for the community to gather, collaborate, and celebrate. The lobby establishes a dramatic entry and connects the two intersecting rectangular volumes representing the library and a community hall. On the ground floor, a power wall and flexible shelving reinforce a retail look and mentality, while self-serve and staff kiosks replace a traditional circulation desk. Beyond the lobby a glass partition with a graphic film shows the way to the children's area. Expansive windows on the first floor in the adult collection and community living room offer views to the foliage of the library's park-like setting and reinforce the theme of transparency and connectivity.

e

f

g

Project LIBRARY IN RUINS
Sunyao Old Village <u>Architects</u> Atelier XI <u>Address</u>
Sunyao Old Village, Xiuwu County, China <u>Client</u>
Xiuwu County <u>Completion</u> 2021 <u>Size</u> 66 m² <u>Type</u>
<u>of library</u> Public <u>Reading seats</u> 20

a

Atelier XI presents a duet of intertwined memories in this building: On the one hand, it combines cave dwellings, barren hills, and earthen walls; on the other, it becomes an abstract sculptural space that grows out of the terrain and rises into the sky. The undulating outline of the roof echoes the terrain and distant mountains, and the roof's surface naturally forms an outdoor terrace and slide for children. The interior space functions not only as a staggered library, but also as a small projection room. On the north and south façades, small custom-built windows puncture the concrete wall. These irregularly shaped openings create a play of shadows during the day and a backdrop of sparkling lights at night.

b

c

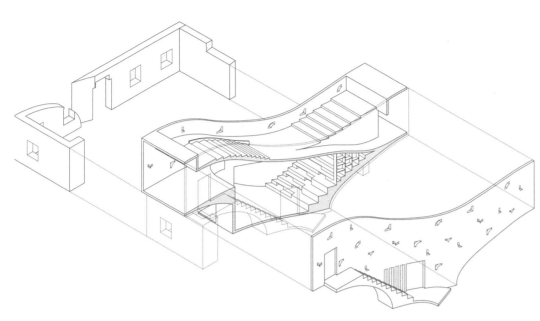

d

e

Project DRUMMONDVILLE PUBLIC LIBRARY Drummondville **Architecture** Chevalier Morales **Landscape** Civiliti **Address** 425, rue des Forges, Drummondville, Quebec J2B0G4, Canada **Client** City of Drummondville **Completion** 2017 **Size** 5,750 m² **Type of library** Public, with Multimedia **Reading seats** 375

a

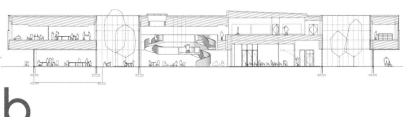

b

c d

Drummondville Public Library is an open and democratic space, a civic facility, and agent of sustainable change. It offers an ambitious public program: a variety of books and digital collections, as well as spaces for reading, social services, stage performances, children's camps, gardens, and access to an outdoor skating rink linked to a geothermal system. Multiple entrances animate the building and welcome everyone into the central foyer filled with natural light. The library is a bright community hub anchored to its context. The curved structure, glass envelope, and spiral staircase are inspired by the City of Drummondville: its Saint-François river, local culture, industry, and hydroelectric power, a key source of renewable energy.

e

f

g

h

Project LIBRARY GUNDELSHEIM Gundelsheim Architecture Schlicht Lamprecht Kern Architekten Address Bachstraße 7, 96163 Gundelsheim, Germany Client City of Gundelsheim Completion 2020 Size 320 m² Type of library Public Reading seats 10 Original building Barn, 19th century

a

The basic urban planning idea for the library is based on the regionally familiar triad of a Franconian farm ensemble: house – stable – barn. The dissolved two-sided structure of the farm was restored, the familiar images of the village center were taken up. The existing residential barn was renovated. A new double gable barn was built where the barn once stood, integrating the existing barn. The library opens to the public space through a new reading courtyard. Mobile shelving allows all areas to be used flexibly as event spaces. The children's library also serves as a group room for the local forest kindergarten. Authentic and natural materials such as wood, stone, and plaster contribute to a familiar appearance.

b

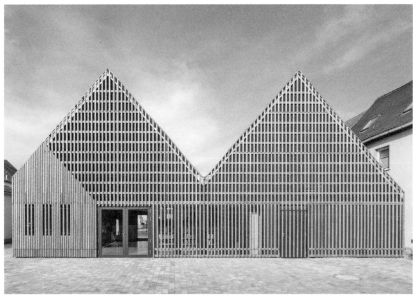

c

d

e
Ground floor plan and section

f
Gallery reading area, former
chicken coop
g
Children's library

95

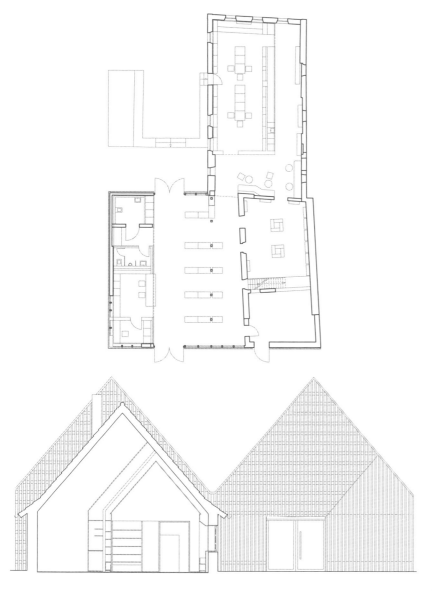

e

f g

LES DOMINICAINS DE
COLMAR

Colmar

Ameller Dubois

a
Entrance courtyard between
historical building and extension

96

Project LES DOMINICAINS DE COLMAR
Colmar Architecture Ameller Dubois, Stefan
Manciulescu Address 1, place des Martyrs-de-
la-Résistance, Colmar, France Client City of
Colmar Completion 2022 Size 3,400 m² Type of
library Public, with Manuscripts Reading seats
50 Original building Cloister, 1300

a

b
Ground floor, first floor and
second floor plan

c
Reading room
d
Museum with books from the
Middle Ages to the 18th century

97

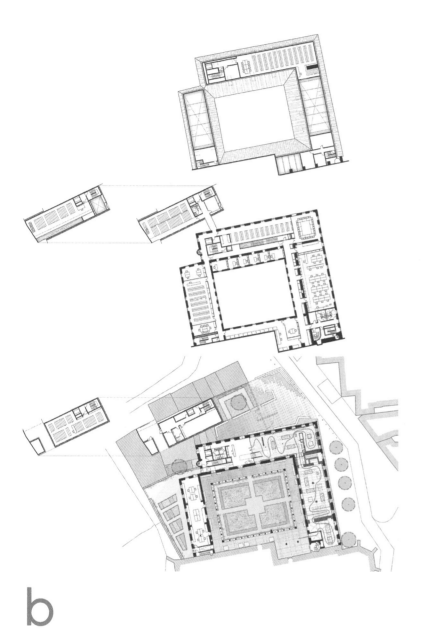

b

cd

The renovation and extension of the 13th century
Dominican Library now provides the city with an exceptional place to house and exhibit one of the most
important and prestigious collections of old books in
Europe. The project has allowed not only the careful
restoration of the Dominican convent and cloister, but
also the conservation and preservation of the graphic
and written documents of inestimable value. The convent, meticulously restored and freed from the many
mutilations it had undergone over the years, in order
to recover its original essence, was joined by a contemporary annex in burnt wood, designed to house documents of lesser prestige; a completely transparent
walkway connects the two buildings.

e

f

gh

Project ARCHITECTURE LIBRARY Bangkok Architecture Department of ARCHITECTURE Lighting Designer APLD Address 254 Phayathai Road, Bangkok, Thailand Client Faculty of Architecture, Chulalongkorn University Completion 2019 Size 1,260 m² Reading seats 234 Type of library University with Architecture Collection

a

b

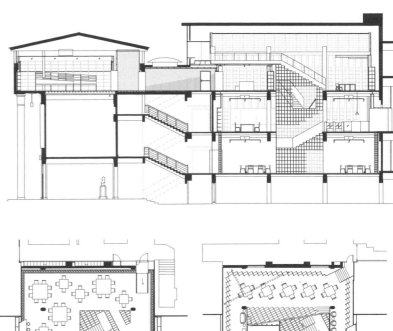

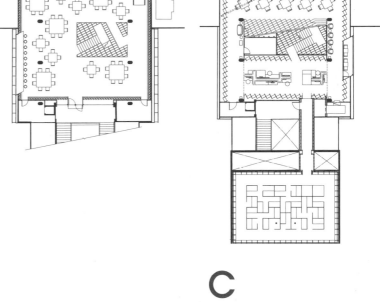

c

The project has expanded the meaning of a library in the digital age, during which the idea that people come to libraries to only read books could become obsolete. The library's entire programing has been reworked. The library is to be a place for exchanging ideas and exploring knowledge not only through books but through different kinds of media. The design has integrated a variety of new programs into the new library. They range from a co-working space, an exhibition space, an experimental art space, to an area for occasional lectures where the library becomes a platform for dialogs and interactions, and it includes not only physical books as sources of knowledge and inspiration but also digital media, movies, exhibitions, etc.

ARCHITECTURE LIBRARY,
CHULALONGKORN
UNIVERSITY

d

Pixel steps usable as auditorium

and movie theater

102

d

e

fg

Project TONAMI PUBLIC LIBRARY
Tonami Architecture Kazuhiko Mashiko & MIKAMI
Architects; Oshida Architects & Engineers
Address 4–1 Saiwai, Tonami, Japan Client City of
Tonami Completion 2020 Size 3,343 m² Type of
library Public Reading seats 272

a

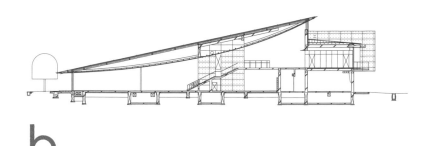

b

cd

The Tonami Public Library was built in an area where once various grains were produced to support Kaga Hyakumangoku – this refers to the measure of wealth the Kaga region attained during the rule of the Maeda clan The architects transformed its history to a new concept: a one-roomed library under the large, gently corrugated roof. They wanted to make this library a new landmark of Tonami, a symbol of its citizens' culture. All visitors are enveloped by the warmth of the dense wooden ceiling and the soft natural light streaming in through the high windows. The ground and first floors are connected by stairs on two sides, and the first floor overlooks the ground floor, which is carpeted with a mosaic of the city's flower, the tulip.

ef

g

h

Project TINGBJERG LIBRARY
Tingbjerg <u>Architecture</u> Cobe <u>Interior</u> Rune
Fjord Studio <u>Landscape</u> Kragh & Berglund
<u>Address</u> Skolesiden 4, 2700 Brønshøj-Husum,
Denmark <u>Client</u> City of Copenhagen, SAB, and
FSB <u>Completion</u> 2018 <u>Size</u> 1,500 m² <u>Type of</u>
<u>library</u> Public <u>Reading seats</u> 18

a

b

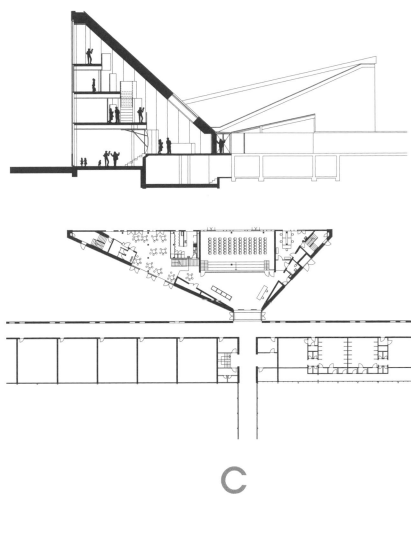

c

Tingbjerg was envisioned as a modernistic suburban garden city just outside Copenhagen, designed with the best intentions of providing high-quality housing. Unfortunately, today, the neighborhood ranks on the Danish government's official list of marginalized crime-ridden areas and is stigmatized by negative media coverage. The library is part of an ambitious strategy to revive the area and restore a sense of pride. A local community center and an iconic learning and knowledge center offer a place for the residents to meet across cultural barriers. Through the large windows within the open frame, the library is designed to project the activity of the building and the lives of the residents of Tingbjerg onto the surrounding area.

TINGBJERG LIBRARY

d
Detail of façade
e
Room for events

f
Reading desks
g
Aerial view

110

de

fg

h

ROBERT L. BOGOMOLNY
LIBRARY

Baltimore, MD

Behnisch Architekten

a
Main entrance

112

Project ROBERT L. BOGOMOLNY LIBRARY
Baltimore, MD Architecture Behnisch
Architekten Landscape Core Studio Design
Address 1420 Maryland Ave Baltimore, MD
21201, USA Client University of Baltimore,
University of Maryland Completion 2018 Size
5,388 m² Type of library University Reading
seats 655 Original building Henry Powell
Hopkins and Associates, 1966

a

The transformation of the Robert L. Bogomolny Library respects the memory and history of the original library design – that of the "floating box" – while simultaneously modernizing it to meet contemporary research, scholarship, archival and environmental demands. To the west of the building there is now a new academic and public space with the addition of a glass hall. The geometry of this addition differentiates the new construction from the existing building while retaining the elemental simplicity of the original floating box. Inside, the glass hall promotes interior circulation, provides the original floor plate with daylight and creates new informal study and meeting perches within its enclosure.

b

c

d

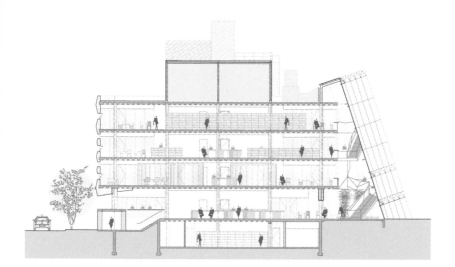

f

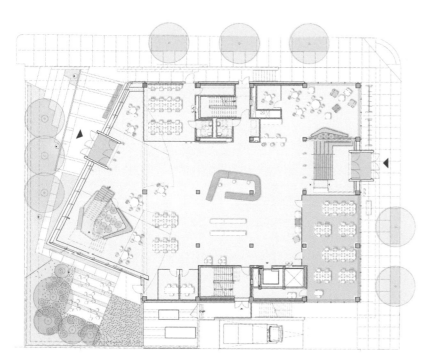

e

UNIVERSITY LIBRARY
EMDEN

Emden

UKW Innenarchitekten

a
Individual work stations

116

Project <u>UNIVERSITY LIBRARY EMDEN</u>
Emden <u>Architecture</u> UKW Innenarchitekten
<u>Signage</u> Studio Aha!, <u>Address</u> Constantiaplatz
4, 26723 Emden, Germany <u>Client</u> Hochschule
Emden/Leer <u>Completion</u> 2018 <u>Size</u> 1,600 m² <u>Type</u>
<u>of library</u> University <u>Reading seats</u> 230 <u>Original</u>
<u>building</u> ARGE FH Ostfriesland, 1981

a

b

The renovation of the library building of the University of Applied Sciences Emden/Leer from the 1980s transformed it conceptually and atmospherically into an innovative learning space. The cladding of the stair railings creates a calm atmosphere, both visually and acoustically. The pale pink of the cladding, the gray-green of the exposed concrete surfaces, and the colorfulness of the furniture corresponds with the existing exposed brickwork. The anthracite-colored media and white service furniture such as the central information counter support orientation. The reduction of the media inventory has created a variety of different learning and working spaces.

UNIVERSITY LIBRARY
EMDEN

c
Seminar room
d
Group workplaces

e
Section and ground floor plan

118

c d

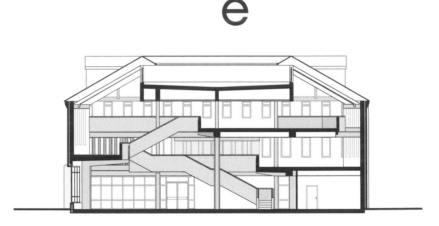

e

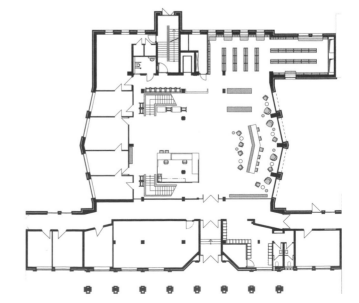

F

<u>Project</u> ASIA ART ARCHIVE
Hong Kong <u>Architecture</u> LAAB Architects
<u>Address</u> 11/F, Hollywood Centre, 233 Hollywood
Road, Sheung Wan, Hong Kong, China <u>Client</u> Asia
Art Archive <u>Completion</u> 2022 <u>Size</u> 450 m² <u>Type</u>
<u>of library</u> Art Archive <u>Reading seats</u> 4

a

Located in Sheung Wan in Hong Kong, the new home of Asia Art Archive required a complete rethinking of its original site to expand the event space as well as to accommodate ten years of archival growth. Departing from the conventional image of an archive as a white space, the new design embraces an open, flexible plan with a warm color palette making the space welcoming for everyone. Originally occupying the center of the library, the bookshelves have been rearranged to line the entire space. The spatial reconfiguration has expanded the collection capacity by 63 percent and the event space by 60 percent. The wooden shelves also work as an exhibition system. The new design commits to sustainability by using natural materials.

b

c

d

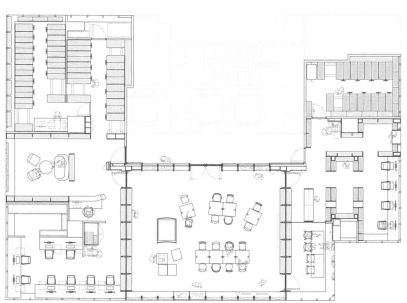

e

f g

MADISON PUBLIC LIBRARY
– PINNEY BRANCH   Madison, WI   OPN Architects   a
                                                            Anji Play is the concept of
                                                            the children's library   124

Project MADISON PUBLIC LIBRARY – PINNEY BRANCH
Madison, WI Architecture OPN Architects
Address 516 Cottage Grove Road, Madison, WI
53716, USA Client City of Madison Completion
2020 Size 1,900 m² Type of library Public, with
artist residency

a

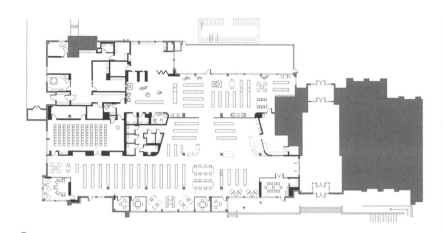

b

c d

The new Pinney Library offers a warm, welcoming environment that promotes literacy through play. The inclusive design uses natural materials and light to create an immediate sense of warmth and connect with many cultures represented by Pinney's diverse neighbors. The 1,900 square-meter space includes a flexible 250-person program room, expanded adult, young adult and children's collections, updated technology, a patio for events and programing, quiet reading and study areas, and a drive-through book drop-off. Within the children's area a playlab offers a flexible space for children to create their own story and environment, incorporating elements of the educational philosophy Anji Play.

MADISON PUBLIC LIBRARY
– PINNEY BRANCH

e
Inside the library
f
Study and reading area

g
Centrally located
service desks
h
Children's area

126

ef

gh

<u>Project</u> WATER DROP LIBRARY
Huizhou City <u>Architecture</u> 3andwich Design
<u>Landscape</u> TOPOS Landscape Architects
<u>Lighting</u> Guangzhu International Lighting Design
<u>Address</u> Shuangyue Bay, Huizhou, China <u>Client</u>
Huizhou Shuangyue Bay Real Estate <u>Completion</u>
2022 <u>Size</u> 450 m² <u>Type of library</u> Public <u>Reading</u>
<u>seats</u> 50

a

b

The architects wanted the building to coexist with the site, so it respects the environment but has its own character. In order to get the best view, the library is hidden at the end of the hill by using the height difference of the terrain. The architectural modeling emphasizes simple geometric shapes – circle, square and straight lines. The roof section is bowl-shaped, and the transparent glass in the reading area gives the roof the appearance of floating. The bowl roof is also a pool, below which is the main building. The interior is composed of a group of dramatic spaces with a sense of sequence, light and dark, opening and closing overlapping.

C

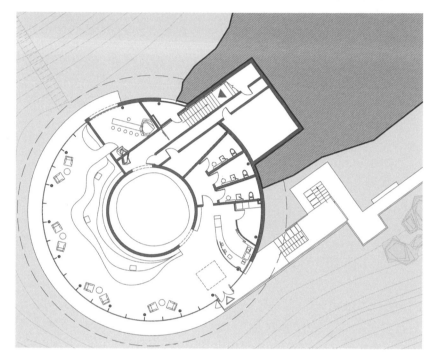

d

ef

FLINT PUBLIC LIBRARY   Flint, MI   OPN Architects   a
Windows and re-clad fins
reflect surrounding
mid-century buildings   132

<u>Project</u> FLINT PUBLIC LIBRARY
Flint, MI <u>Architecture</u> OPN Architects <u>Address</u>
1026 E. Kearsley Street, Flint, MI 48503, USA
<u>Client</u> Flint Public Library District <u>Completion</u>
2022 <u>Size</u> 8,730 m² <u>Type of library</u> Public, with
State Archives <u>Original building</u> Sulho Alexander
Nurmi, 1958

a

The purpose of this library was to transform, renew, revitalize, and reinvent its 1950s building into a modern and flexible beacon for learning and hope. It was remade from the inside out, transforming it into an equitable, confident, and aspirational place both for and of its community. While maintaining the original footprint of the building, the 8730-square-meter interior was reconfigured to include new openings between the first and second floors. Windows were added and replaced. Exterior architectural fins, both new and old, with the latter being re-clad, reflect the surrounding mid-century buildings that comprise the cultural campus on which the library sits.

b

c

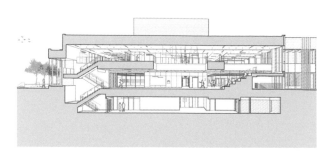

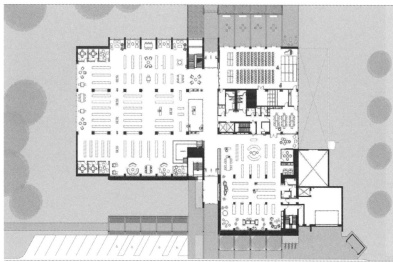

d

Project PHIVE CIVIC CENTER Parramatta <u>Architecture</u> Manuelle Gautrand Architecture; Designinc; Lacoste & Stevenson <u>Address</u> 5 Paramatta Square, Parramatta NSW 2150, Australia <u>Client</u> Parramatta City Council <u>Completion</u> 2023 <u>Size</u> 15,000 m² <u>Type of library</u> Public, with Multimedia and Manuscripts <u>Reading seats</u> 400

a

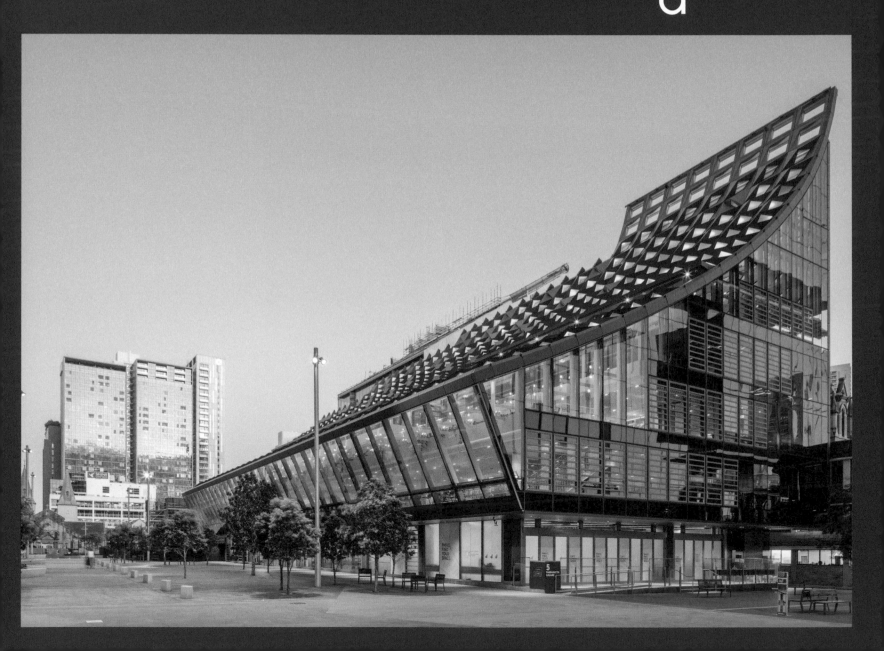

b
Stairs connecting the two floors

c
Ground and second
floor plan and Manuelle
Gautrand's drawing

137

b

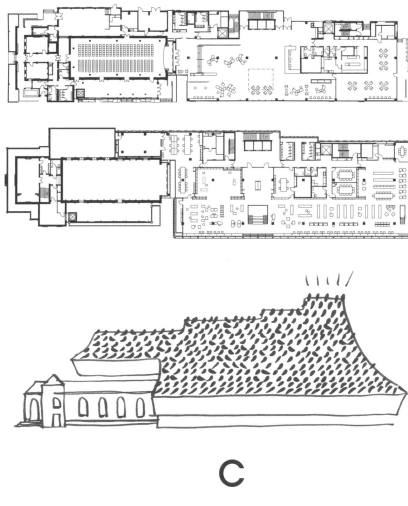

c

This project is a public and cultural facility featuring community and exhibition spaces as well as the City of Parramatta's Council Chamber. A place where locals and visitors can meet, discover, learn and share. Its triangular outline is shaped according to the course of the sun, to allow the sun to shine on the square all year round. The roof curves slightly toward the top of the new civic spire, with colors moving from dark to light. The envelope is a highly sustainable skin that filters light and views, creating a poetic atmosphere for the exterior and interior of the project. Inside this chiseled volume, a cascade of levels faces the square in a kind of giant amphitheater. The higher one climbs, the more narrow and intimate the spaces become.

d

ef

g

Project ANIMU MEDIA LIBRARY
Porto-Vecchio Architecture Dominique Coulon &
associés Landscape Bruno Kubler Address Voie
Romaine, 20137 Porto-Vecchio, France Client
City of Porto-Vecchio Completion 2022 Size
2,805 m² Type of library Public, with Multimedia
Reading seats 185

a

b

c d

The principle of the Animu Media Library in Corsica is to preserve the landscape, therefore the shape of the building is echoing its surroundings. The building appears to float above the landscape, with as little impact on it as possible. Its curves are designed to skirt the trees and rocks. A ramp leads users to a special garden, conceived as a place for outdoor reading, while a summer bar slides into the space below the building to create a shaded terrace. The underside of the building is designed as a separate area. Inside, the main feature is the fluidity of the space. There is a lot of natural light and the bays offer a choice of panoramic views.

ef g

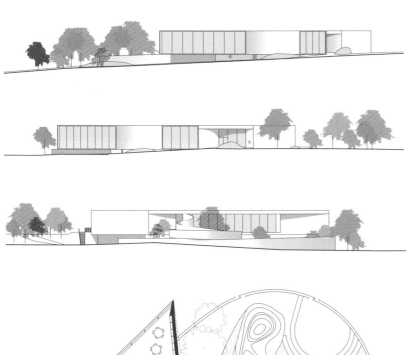

i

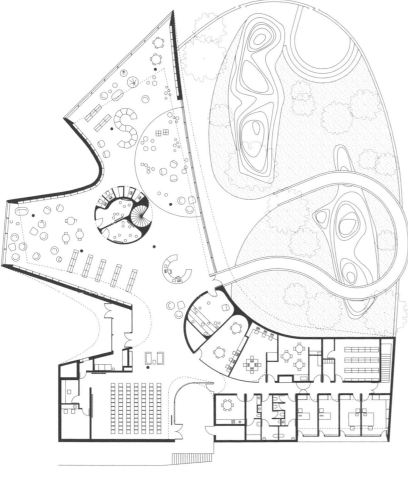

h

Project ILSE WALLENTIN HAUS, UNIVERSITÄT FÜR BODENKULTUR Vienna <u>Architecture</u> SWAP Architektur <u>Address</u> Peter-Jordan-Straße 82, Vienna, Austria <u>Client</u> Boku Universität für Bodenkultur <u>Completion</u> 2020 <u>Size</u> 5,000 m² <u>Type of library</u> University <u>Reading seats</u> 100

a

The Boku University needed a larger library and seminar center. SWAP Architektur in cooperation with DELTA convinced with a building in visible timber construction. It is a distinctive building with untreated façade surface. The grid of the façade is continued inside the entrance level and the library in the ceiling construction, making the supporting structure a design element. Floor-to-ceiling glazing establishes a dialogue between interior and the surroundings. By opening individual glass elements, the terrace can be accessed as a meeting place. The four-story wooden building was constructed from prefabricated glulam elements; the base in contact with the ground as well as the staircase are made of reinforced concrete.

b

C

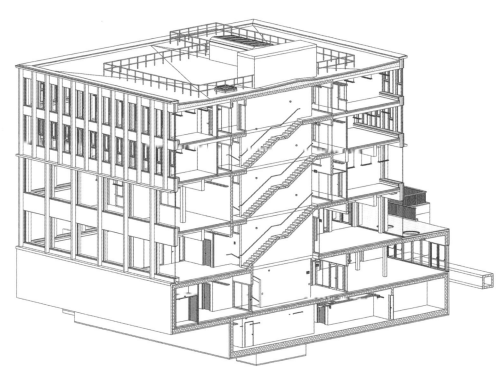

d

e

<u>Project</u> 164_PUBLIC LIBRARY
Veggiano <u>Architecture</u> MIDE architetti <u>Address</u>
Via S. Francesco, 9/A, 35030 Veggiano, Italy
<u>Client</u> Municipality of Veggiano <u>Completion</u>
2020 <u>Size</u> 300 m² <u>Type of library</u> Public, with
Multimedia and Music <u>Reading seats</u> 7

a

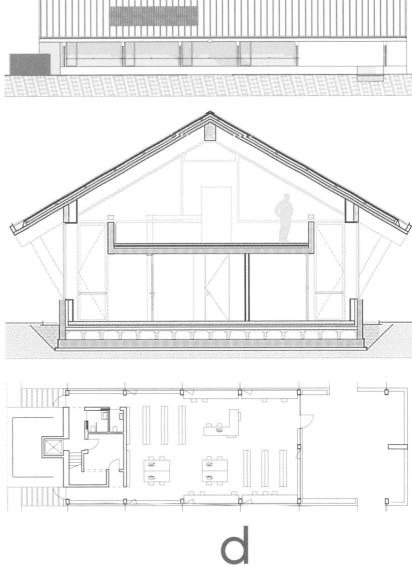

d

b c

The new library is located in an area with a public park. The final result is a building surrounded by greenery, where it is pleasant to spend time. The choice to place the building parallel to the main road is motivated by the desire to realize a representative and distinctive building that welcomes the citizens. The chance to realize a new library was considered an opportunity to design a public building that serves as an identifying object for the community. The building faces the rural environment, characterized by farm buildings with pitched roofs and arcades. The new library looks to the future: a Near Zero Energy Building (NZEB), characterized by a wooden structure that provides a welcoming and warm atmosphere.

e

f

g

h

YUSUHARA COMMUNITY
LIBRARY

Yusuhara

Kengo Kuma & Associates

a
Façade and main entrance

152

Project YUSUHARA COMMUNITY LIBRARY
Yusuhara <u>Architecture</u> Kengo Kuma &
Associates <u>Address</u> Yusuhara Town, Takaoka
County, Kochi, Japan <u>Client</u> City of Yusuhara
<u>Completion</u> 2018 <u>Size</u> 1,931 m² <u>Type of library</u>
Public

a

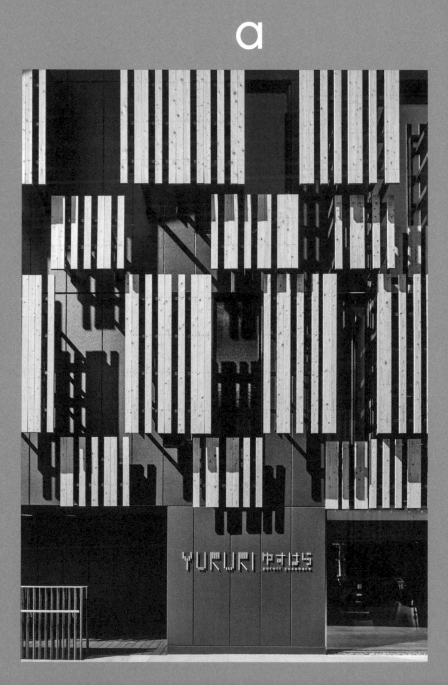

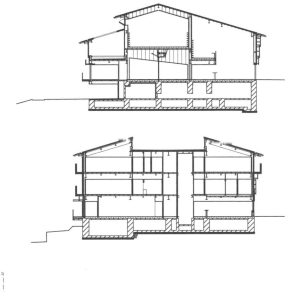

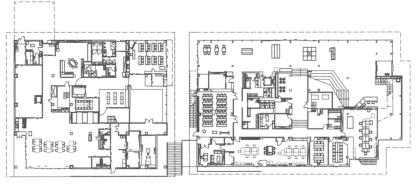

d

b c

Yusuhara, a town on the border of Kochi and Ehime, is often described as a village above the clouds. Kengo Kuma & Associates built a complex of buildings, including a library and welfare facilities, using mainly cedar from the woods surrounding the town. With a sports facility and daycare center on the other side of the lawn, the site has become the heart of the town, fostering interaction and communication between generations of locals. The structure is a mix of steel and cedar, expressing a forest with sunlight filtering through the leaves. Instead of a large flat floor, the floor is undulating and can be used as a stage for events. In the library, everyone takes off their shoes to feel the warmth of the cedar floor and read books anywhere in the space.

e

f

g

h

Project CONVENT OF THE SACRED HEART LIBRARY
New York, NY <u>Architecture</u> 1100 Architect
<u>Address</u> 1 E 91st St, New York, NY 10128, <u>Client</u>
Convent of the Sacred Heart <u>Completion</u> 2019
<u>Size</u> 2,100 m² <u>Type of library</u> Children's library
<u>Reading seats</u> 94 <u>Original building</u> J. Armstrong
Stenhouse and C. P. H. Gilbert, 1917

a

b

1100 Architect refurbished the library at Convent
of the Sacred Heart, an all-girls K-12 school on
Manhattan's Upper East Side. Located in an early 20th
century landmarked building, the project integrates
modern design elements while maintaining the library's
historic character. The design creates a welcoming
environment through use of color, texture, and
pattern. Modular furniture allows for large and small
group settings, and naturally lit study nooks provide
space for individual learning. This refurbishment is part
of an ongoing relationship between 1100 Architect and
Convent of the Sacred Heart, where the office has
completed construction on a new science facility and
maker-space.

Convent of the Sacred
Heart Library

c
Study nooks provide space for
private study and focus

d
Floor plan and site plan

158

c

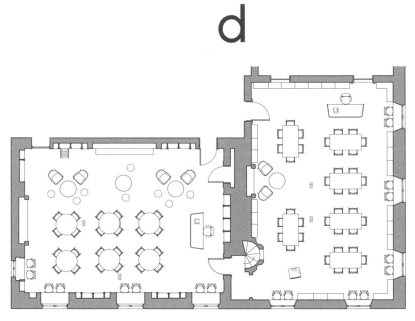

d

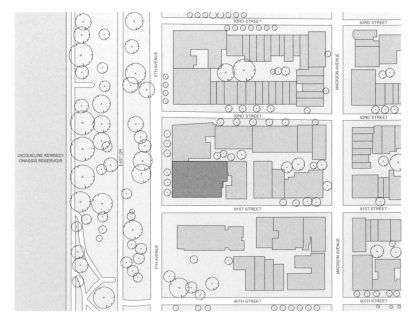

e
Modular furniture allows
for large and small group
settings

159

e

Project STUDIUM
Strasbourg Architecture Jean-Pierre LOTT–
architecte Address 2, rue Blaise Pascal,
67000 Strasbourg, France Client Université
de Strasbourg Completion 2022 Size 12,000 m²
Type of library University, with Multimedia,
Music and Manuscripts Reading seats 700

a

Studium was born from the desire of the University of Strasbourg to have a different building, both a library and a learning center, an environment that would encourage mingling, meetings and exchanges. The building marks the entrance to the campus coming from the city, it gives its first impression. The building offers a glazed ground floor inviting to enter, surmounted by a body with sinuous shapes expressing movement, lightness, metaphors of concentration and reading. The transparent base on the public space allows a view of the spaces on the ground floor. The façade protects the building according to the path of the sun to ensure temperature control, while guaranteeing the necessary supply of light and views of the city.

b

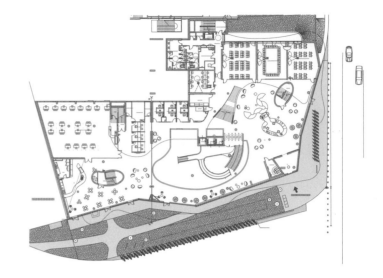

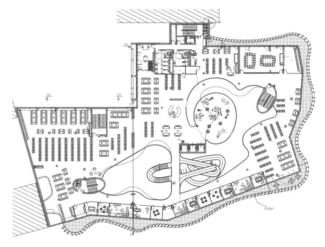

cd

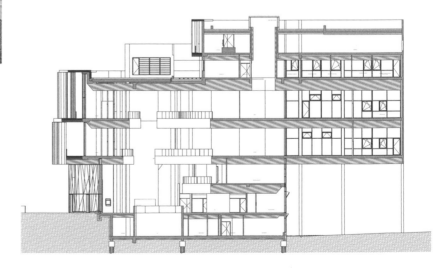

e

Project BIBLIOTHEK DER WIRTSCHAFTSWISSENSCHAFTEN Freiburg Architecture fuchs.maucher. architekten. Artist atelier JAK Address Rempartstraße 10–16, 79098 Freiburg, Germany Client Vermögen und Bau BW Amt Freiburg Completion 2020 Size 1,925 m² Type of library University Reading seats 125

a

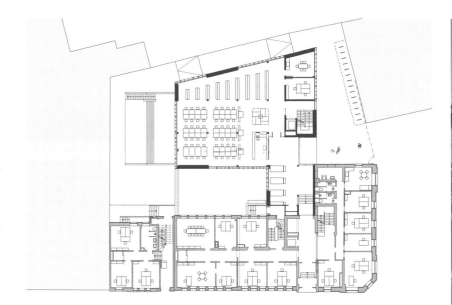

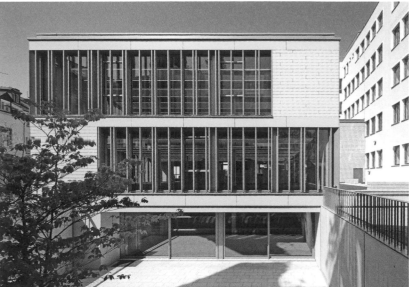

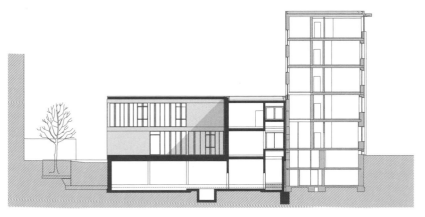

b

c d

The library building is divided into three levels. On the
entrance floor there is the public-intensive area of the
information desk, the booking area, the research area,
and the book lending area. On the upper floor, visually connected to the ground floor via a skylight, is the
quiet reading and study area. In the basement, there
are the archives, the parlatory and the adjoining group
rooms. A low courtyard gives this area natural lighting
despite its location in the basement. The reserved materiality and color palette of the surfaces result from
the idea that books and people already provide variety
and color for the rooms. The only colorful element is
the artwork in the light well, which consists of poetry
verses in the form of colorful letter clusters.

BIBLIOTHEK DER
WIRTSCHAFTSWISSEN-
SCHAFTEN

e
Book return desk

f
Artwork in the building

166

e

f

g

h

<u>Project</u> CIVAC LINEAR PARK
Jiutepec <u>Architecture</u> Rozana Montiel Estudio
de Arquitectura; Claudia Rodríguez <u>Landscape</u>
Brenda Landeros <u>Address</u> Av. 50 Metros 44, San
Isidro, Jiutepec, Morelos, 62578, Mexico <u>Client</u>
SEDATU <u>Completion</u> 2022 <u>Size</u> 2,100 m² <u>Type of</u>
<u>library</u> Public <u>Reading seats</u> 48

a

CIVAC Linear Park is an infrastructure and urban renewal project in Jiutepec. The project integrates 1.15 kilometers of Linear Park, a civic center that houses the public institutions of the municipality and a new skate park. The main design premise is based on recovering the identity of the local landscape. Some of the more than 50 years old trees were integrated into the architecture. The base of Texcal stone generates a series of platforms, terraces and galleries that connect the path of the buildings with courtyards, gardens and resting areas. The main material that was used is sand-colored pigmented concrete. The administrative program is complemented by a library, a cafeteria, different workshops and a children's playground.

b

cd

d

e

f

Project HET PREDIKHEREN Mechelen <u>Architecture</u> Korteknie Stuhlmacher Architecten; Callebaut Architecten; Bureau Bouwtechniek <u>Address</u> Goswin de Stassartstraat 88, 2800 Mechelen, Belgium <u>Client</u> City of Mechelen <u>Completion</u> 2019 <u>Size</u> 5,840 m² <u>Type of library</u> Public <u>Reading seats</u> 150 <u>Original building</u> Dominican Monastery, 1650/1720

a

b

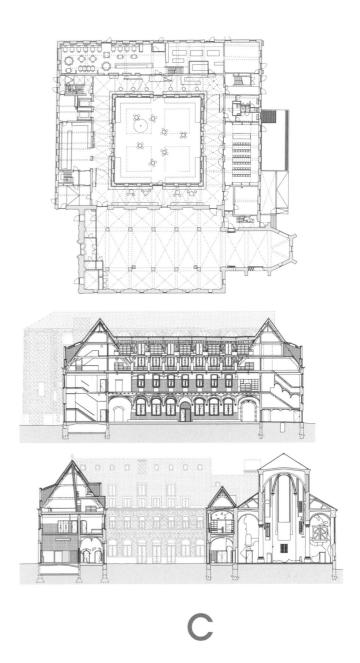

c

The baroque Dominican convent was built in 1650, decon-
secrated in the late 18th century and was used as bar-
racks, a school and a military hospital. In 2010, the city
of Mechelen decided to restore this impressive ruin
and to create a public library in its monumental rooms.
The charm of the ruin is the conceptual framework of
the restoration and the new use. The damaged original
fabric remains visible on the exterior and interior. The
installation of the rooms avoided structural adjust-
ments as much as possible. The concept of a sustainable installation and the manner of renovation, refurbishment and insulation are geared towards this. The
various historical layers with their different textures
and discolorations are part of the new spaces.

d

e

fg

CITY LIBRARY KARBEN   Karben   Marie-Theres Deutsch
Architekten   a
Entrance axis   176

<u>Project</u> CITY LIBRARY KARBEN
Karben <u>Architecture</u> Marie-Theres Deutsch
Architekten <u>Address</u> Bahnhofstraße 197, 61184
Karben, Germany <u>Client</u> Magistrate of the
City Karben <u>Completion</u> 2021 <u>Size</u> 430 m² <u>Type
of library</u> Public <u>Reading seats</u> 50

a

b

The so-called Neue Mitte Karben is built on the edge of the city of Karben next to the commuter train station. The public transport provides the connection to the Frankfurt/Main exurbs. 2018 the city rented the first floor with 430 cubic meters in the building. There, in addition to commerce, a cultural center was created for everyone by Marie-Theres Deutsch Architekten: it offers a library including music rooms and game consoles. Film events can host up to 120 people There are fixed working group spaces and informal spaces on 60 meters long benches. The terrace offers an outdoor cinema, the lounge offers daily press and magazines. The 30-meter entrance axis can accommodate 60 people for seated dining at special receptions.

C

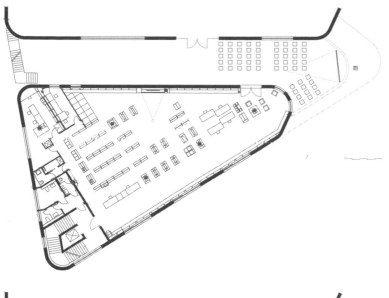

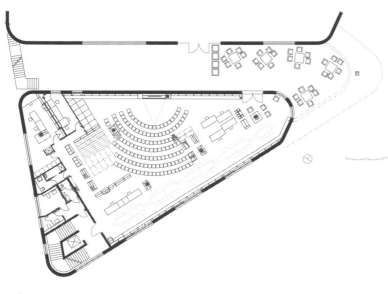

d

ef

Project LA CONTEMPORAINE
Nanterre Architecture Atelier Bruno Gaudin
Architectes Address Campus Universitaire
de Nanterre, 92050 Nanterre, France Client
EPAURIF Completion 2021 Size 6,790 m² Type
of library University, with Multimedia and
Manuscripts Reading seats 102

a

As a foundational element in an emerging neighborhood, the building makes the institution visible in the urban fabric. A tower on top addresses the wider surroundings. This unitary volume, made of brick, a homogeneous and durable material, is hollowed out according to the needs and specificities of the interior spaces. Special attention has been paid to the building envelope with a climatic approach to manage energy costs and supplies. The building's multidisciplinary functions make it both a place of documentation and an educational tool, with permanent and temporary exhibition rooms, consultation and work rooms, educational workshops, classrooms and training rooms.

b

cd

e

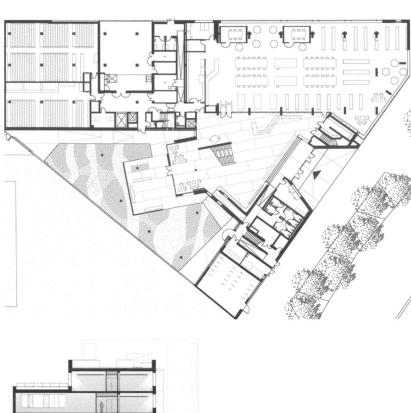

f

g

Project <u>BRIXEN PUBLIC LIBRARY</u>
Brixen <u>Architecture</u> Carlana Mezzalira
Pentimalli <u>Address</u> Piazza del Duomo 4, 39042
Brixen, Italy <u>Client</u> Municipality of Brixen
<u>Completion</u> 2022 <u>Size</u> 3,013 m² <u>Type of library</u>
Public <u>Reading seats</u> 150

a

b

The new public library of Brixen is conceived as a small
social infrastructure in which the relationship between
old and new is specific and inseparable. The peculiarities
of the urban context and the needs of a public building
open to the community were the starting point for
the design. This contemporary intervention is capable
of looking to the future of the city, integrating itself
quietly into the urban fabric and seeking a profound
dialogue with the preexisting structures. This architecture is more than just a library: It is a social and
sustainable device designed to welcome and generate
human relationships.

c

d

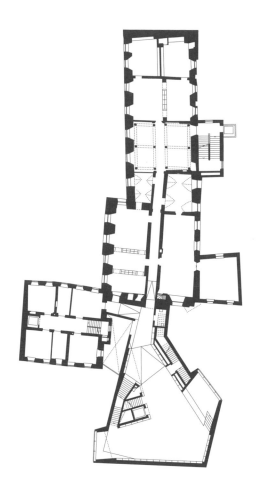

e

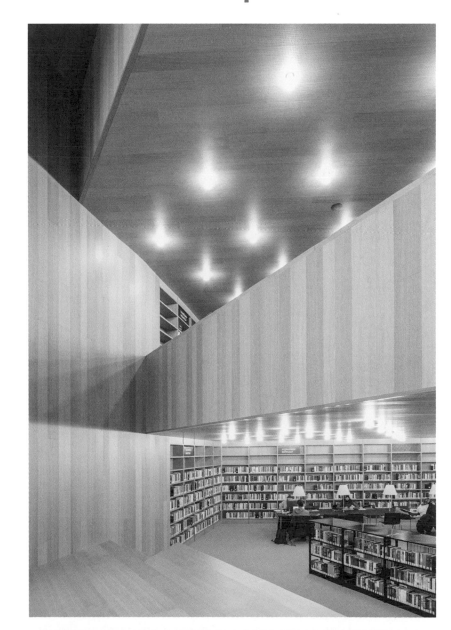

f

HELSINKI CENTRAL
LIBRARY OODI

Helsinki

ALA Architects

a
View on the library

188

Project HELSINKI CENTRAL LIBRARY OODI
Helsinki Architecture ALA Architects Address
Töölönlahdenkatu 4, Helsinki, Finland Client City
of Helsinki Completion 2018 Size 17,062 m² Type
of library Public

a

b

c

The new library in the heart of Helsinki consists almost entirely of public space. The building is a highly functional addition to local urban life. It offers a technically and spatially flexible platform for cutting edge library operations and acts as the citizens' shared living room. The key concept of the design is the interplay between the three distinct public floors created by the building's bridge-like structure: an active, constantly updated ground floor with a restaurant, multi-purpose hall and cinema; a serene library landscape on the top floor; and an enclosed volume in between them, containing a fab lab, reading room, group working areas, game rooms, and recording and editing studios.

d

e

f

g

GABRIEL GARCÍA
MÁRQUEZ LIBRARY

Barcelona

SUMA arquitectura

a
Agora showcase

192

Project GABRIEL GARCÍA MÁRQUEZ LIBRARY
Barcelona <u>Architecture</u> SUMA arquitectura
<u>Address</u> C/ del Treball, 219, 08020 Barcelona,
Spain <u>Client</u> BIMSA Municipality of Barcelona
<u>Completion</u> 2022 <u>Size</u> 4,294 m² <u>Type of library</u>
Public <u>Reading seats</u> 279

a

The unique district library is presented as a sculptural volume inspired by stacked blocks, sitting on a plaza slightly elevated above the street, its large gaps and voids dialoguing with the environment. A central courtyard brings natural light into the heart of the building. The large voids also act as a solar chimney that absorbs solar radiation by heating the air inside, which rises and is ventilated at the top, creating natural ventilation. The structure is a hybrid of wood and steel, maximizing structural efficiency and architectural performance. The building is part of a new production and consumption model where resources and materials are permanently recycled and waste is minimized to the maximum, thus extending the life cycle of the products.

b

c

d

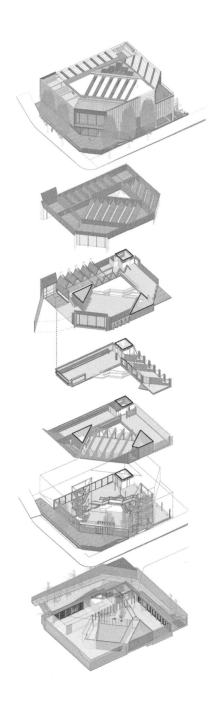

ƒg

e

ÖSTERREICHISCHE
AKADEMIE DER
WISSENSCHAFTEN

Vienna

Riepl Kaufmann Bammer
Architektur

a
View of the shelves and
windows

196

Project ÖSTERREICHISCHE AKADEMIE DER WISSENSCHAFTEN
Vienna <u>Architecture</u> Riepl Kaufmann Bammer Architektur <u>Address</u> Bäckerstraße 19, 1010 Vienna, Austria <u>Client</u> Bundesimmobilien-gesellschaft <u>Completion</u> 2022 <u>Size</u> 508 m² <u>Type of library</u> Science, with historic collection <u>Reading seats</u> 10

a

b

The Österreichische Akademie der Wissenschaften is not represented only by isolated historical buildings, but is now a publicly accessible part of the city. The area has been opened up in a carefully planned manner on all sides, revealing surprising connections and creating a whole out of previously loose parts. The perception of the place is changed through concise, targeted interventions. The redesign gives this important institution the presence it needs in public space. The lost historic library was interpreted in a contemporary way within the framework of the historic substance and offers a stimulating atmosphere for researchers and visitors.

ÖSTERREICHISCHE
AKADEMIE DER
WISSENSCHAFTEN

c
Finished library
d
Before renovation

e
Situation

198

cd

e

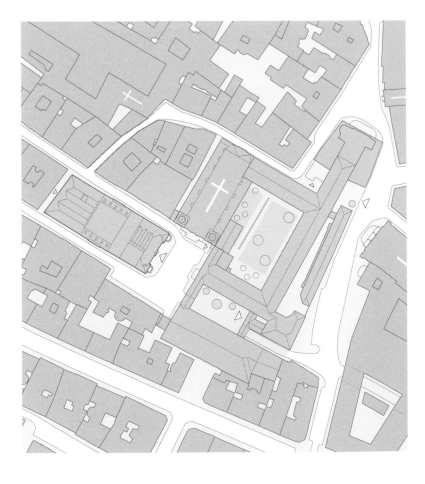

ABU DHABI CHILDREN'S
LIBRARY

Abu Dhabi

CEBRA

a
Front view

200

Project ABU DHABI CHILDREN'S LIBRARY
Abu Dhabi <u>Architecture</u> CEBRA <u>Exhibition</u>
<u>designer</u> Hüttinger <u>Address</u> Sheikh Rashid
Bin Saeed Al Maktoum Street, Abu Dhabi, UAE
<u>Client</u> Department of Culture and Tourism Abu
Dhabi <u>Completion</u> 2019 <u>Size</u> 5,250 m² <u>Type of</u>
<u>library</u> Children <u>Reading seats</u> 12

a

b

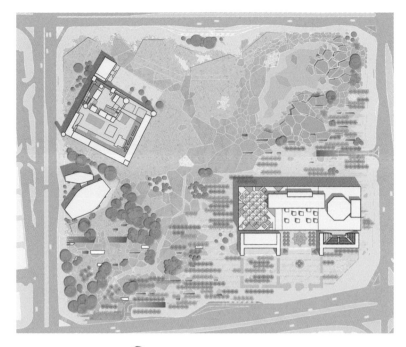

c

CEBRA established the emirate's first children's library in Abu Dhabi's Cultural Foundation Building. The three-floor library surrounds the transparent diagonal atrium and helps to transform the building into a welcoming community space for cultural events and active learning. The library is designed as a life-size pop-up book, where the interiors literally jump out of the stories as a series of themed areas inspired by literature and the diverse nature of the UAE. The design includes spaces for digital creation equipped for children to learn to code and programme simple software, and to record podcasts or even movies. This immersive environment empowers children to explore literature in their own way.

de

f

SECONDARY SCHOOL
LIBRARY AT PANYADEN

Chiang Mai

Chiangmai Life Architects

a
Center with seating

204

Project SECONDARY SCHOOL LIBRARY AT PANYADEN
Chiang Mai Architecture Chiangmai Life Architects Address Hangdong, Chiang Mai 50230, Thailand Client Panyaden International School Completion 2022 Size 392 m² Type of library Children Reading seats 90

a

The Secondary School Library at Panyaden International School was designed to create an inspiring, peaceful and comfortable atmosphere for teenage students to read and study. It provides traditional spaces with tables but also lounge-like spaces with a more relaxed setting decorated with bean bags and pillows. The library has a concentric design with a central oculus, a sunken pod featuring an eye to the sky through the skylight above, surrounded in concentric circles first by built-in small working tables and then by a bamboo archway that houses the main bookshelf section. The library also houses two noise-insulated study rooms for group sessions and a small office for the librarian.

b

c

d

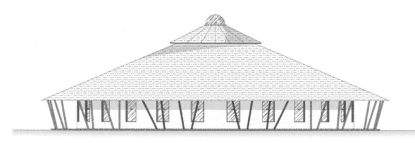

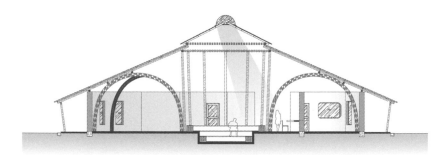

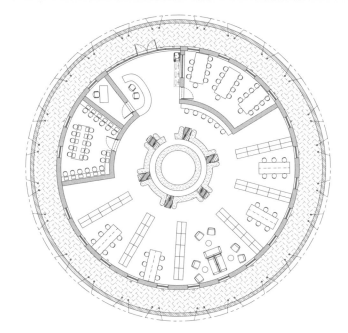

e

f

Project KIRKKONUMMI LIBRARY
Kirkkonummi Architecture JKMM Architects
Address Kirkkotori 1, 02400 Kirkkonummi,
Finnland Client Municipality of Kirkkonummi
Completion 2020 Size 4,700 m² Type of library
Public Reading seats 250 Original building Ola
Hansson, 1982

a

b
Copper shingle cladding and
window front

c
Reading places

d
Copper shingle cladding and
main entrance

209

Together with the nearby open market, the church and library create the civic center of Kirkkonummi. JKMM has designed a 50 meters long sheltered terrace overlooking the churchyard. The copper shingle cladding of the new library, called Fyyri, also relates back to its maritime heritage setting. The 1980s building has been remodeled, doubling its volume, and introducing a large variety of accommodation for community uses as well as exhibition areas. The interiors include bespoke lighting with brass fittings that create warmth. Overall, the building is inspired by its surrounding coastal landscape particularly in the tonality of its interiors. For example, local nature has inspired the choice of subdued colors and of materials like wool.

b

c d

e

f

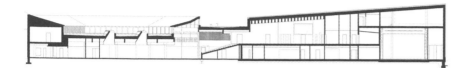

g

h

Project SAMLING
Sagstua Architecture Helen & Hard Address
Sentrumsvegen 22, 2120 Sagstua, Norway Client
Municipality of Nord-Odal Completion 2020 Size
3,000 m² Type of library Public Reading seats
40

a

Samling is a signature building that brings together literature, knowledge, business, people, tradition and history under one roof. The building is relatively compact, with an open atrium in the center. The characteristic radial geometry defines the layout of the building. The cladding of the façades consists of vertical wooden slats. This gives the building an effect of depth and creates a holistic architectural expression. The large glass surfaces of the public spaces create transparency between the inside and the outside. Through the extensive use of wood, the building inspires a more sustainable and responsible society and reflects the cultural heritage of wooden buildings.

b

c

f

de

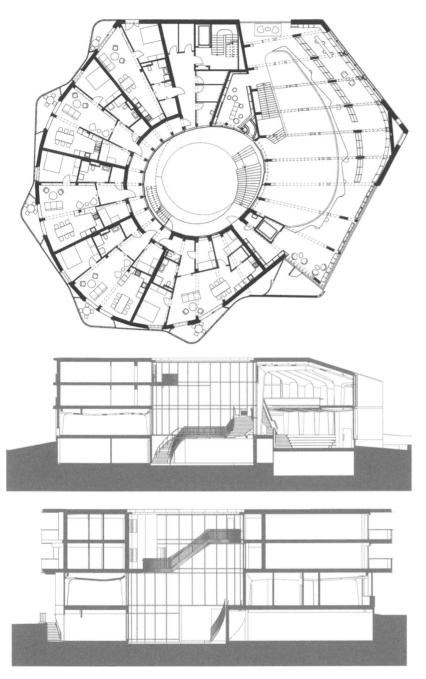

g

h

Project <u>UNIVERSITY LIBRARY GRAZ</u>
Graz <u>Architecture</u> Atelier Thomas Pucher
<u>Address</u> Bahnhofgürtel 77/6, 8020 Graz,
Austria <u>Client</u> Bundesimmobiliengesellschaft
<u>Completion</u> 2019 <u>Size</u> 10,000 m² <u>Type of library</u>
University <u>Reading seats</u> 650 <u>Original Building</u>
1895

a

The Karl Franzens University Library is the largest library in Styria with a stock of four million media. The project includes a lecture hall for 430 students, 650 reading places as well as a study and examination department and administration and storage areas. All functions are executed as independent volumes. The design exposes the historic structure by demolishing a 1970s building section and a connecting structure to the main building. A transparent foyer as a central distribution and event space and a floating beam as an open area for meeting and learning are added to the historic substance. A generous square on the campus creates a link between the law sciences, library, main building and the surrounding university buildings.

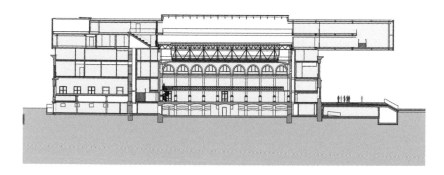

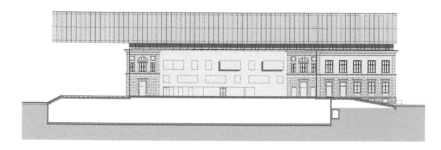

b

c

UNIVERSITY LIBRARY GRAZ   d

Exterior view

e

Inside view

f

Atrium

g

Lecture hall

218

de

fg

Einar Alasken 16–19
Daici Ano, www.fwdinc.jp 32–35
Iwaan Baan, www.iwan.com 188–191: b, c, d
John Bartelstone, www.johnbartelstone.com 28–31: a, d, f, g, h
Alessandra Bello, www.alessandrabello.com 148–151
Moritz Bernoully, www.moritzbernoully.com 176–179
Brett Boardman, www.brettboardman.com 136–139: b, d
Boku, www.boku.ac.at 144–147: a
Patrick Bogner 96–99
Christophe Bourgeois, www.chbourgeois.com 160–163
Didier Boy de la Tour, www.graphisme-photographie.com 36–39
Marco Cappelletti, www.marcocappelletti.com 184–187
Zhang Chao, www.cargocollective.com 84–87
Sanjay Chauhan 44–47: d
Alberto Cosi, www.albertocosi.com 204–207: a, d, f
CreatAR Images, www.creatarimages.com 08–11
Benjamin Drummond 40–43
Bernd Ducke, www.berndducke.de 64–67
Sindre Ellingsen, www.sindreellingsen.com 212–215
Brad Feinknopf, www.feinknopf.com 112–115: a, f
Mikkel Frost, CEBRA 200–203
Marc Goodwin 208–211: c
Jesús Granada, www.jesusgranada.com 192 -195
Rasmus Hjortshøj – COAST Studio, www.rasmushjortshoj.com 108–111
Kouji Horiuchi, www.japs.jp 52–55, 104–107
Kees Hummel 12–15
Hertha Hurnaus 144–147: e
Kawasumi Kobayashi Kenji Photograph Office 152–155
Jens Kirchner, www.jens-kirchner.com 56–59, 116–119
Bruno Klomfar, www.klomfar.com 196–199
Luuk Kramer 172–75
Tom Kurek, www.tomkurekthephotographer.com 76–79
Kuo-min Lee 60–63
Ingeborg F. Lehmann, www.lehmann-fotodesign.de 164–167: c, d, e, f, g, h
Nic Lehoux, www.niclehoux.com 44–47: a, b, c, f, g
Alexandre Massé, www.chevaliermorales.com 88–91: c, d, e, g
David Matthiessen, www.davidmatthiessen.com 112–115: b, c, d
Stefan Meyer 92–95
Alex Michl 80–83: a, 124–127, 132–135
Moving Image Studio 120–123: a, d
Niels Nygaard, www.nielsnygaard.com 68–71
Otto Ng of LAAB 120–123: b, c, f, g
Crystal O'Brien-Kupfner 216–219: d
Sandra Pereznieto, www.pereznieto.com 168–171
Eric Petschek, www.ericpetschek.com 156–159
Eugeni Pons, www.eugenipons.com 140–143
Michael Rebholz, www.mikerebholz.com 80–83: b, c, e, f, g
Markus Roselieb, www.clcarchitects.com 204–207: b, c
Pauliina Salonen 208–211: a, e, h

David Schreyer, www.schreyerdavid.com 216–219: a, c, e, f, g, h
Takuji Shimmura, www.takuji-shimmura.fr 180–183
Shuangyue Bay Real Estate 128–131: a
Jim Stephenson, www.clickclickjim.com 48–51
Parham Taghioff 20–23
Bernhard Tränkle, www.architekturimbild.de 164–167: a
Max Touhey 28–31: c, e
Tuomas Uusheimo, www.uusheimo.com 188–191: a, e, g, 208–211: d, f
Sara Vita, www.saravita.com 136–139: a, e, f, g
Florian Voggeneder 144–147: b, c
Jin Weiqi, www.jinweiqi.top 128–131: b, c, e, f
Adrien Williams, www.adrienwilliams.com 88–91: a, f
W Workspace, www.wisont.wordpress.com 100–103
YHLAA, www.behance.net/iamethanlee.com 24–27

All other pictures were made available by the architects.

The Deutsche Nationalbibliothek lists this publication in the Deutsche Nationalbibliografie; detailed bibliographic data are available on the Internet at http://dnb. dnb.de

ISBN 978-3-03768-293-7
© 2024 by Braun Publishing AG
www.braun-publishing.ch

1st edition 2024

Editor: Editorial Office van Uffelen
Editorial staff and layout:
Katja Löffler, Ilker Önelmis
Graphic concept: STUDIO LZ, Stuttgart
Reproduction: Bild1Druck GmbH, Berlin

Cover front: CreatAR Images
Cover back (from left to right, from above to below):
Kuo-min Lee, Jin Weiqi, Bruno Klomfar